C R O C H

Scrap Granny Crochet™

General Information

Many of the products used in this pattern book can be purchased from local craft, fabric and variety stores, or from the Annie's Attic Needlecraft Catalog *(see Customer Service information on page 16)*.

Contents

Kaleidoscope Colors

Designs by Tammy Hildebrand

SKILL LEVEL

INTERMEDIATE

FINISHED SIZES

Instructions given fit 32- to 34-inch bust (small), 36- to 38-inch bust (medium), 40- to 42-inch bust (large) and 44- to 46-inch bust (X-large). Use specified hook size to achieve desired jacket size.

FINISHED GARMENT MEASUREMENTS

Jacket: 31½ inches (small), 36 inches (medium), 40½ inches (large) and 45 inches (X-large)

Scarf: 4 inches wide x 56½ inches long

MATERIALS

Jacket

- ❑ Lion Brand Microspun light (DK) weight yarn (2.5 oz/70g/ 168 yds/154m per skein):
  - 2 [3, 4, 5] skeins #910-098 French vanilla *(MC)*
  - 5 yds desired color for each motif *(CC)*
- ❑ Size G/6/4mm [H/8/5mm, J/10/6mm, K/10½/6.5mm] crochet hook or size needed to obtain gauge

Scarf

- ❑ Lion Brand Microspun light (DK) weight yarn (2/5 oz/70g/ 168 yds/154m per skein):
  - 1 skein #910-098 French vanilla *(MC)*
  - 5 yds desired color for each motif *(CC)*
- ❑ Size G/6/4mm crochet hook or size needed to obtain gauge

GAUGE

First Motif of Jacket = 3½ [4, 4½, 5] inches square with size G [H, J, K] crochet hook

SPECIAL STITCHES

Open shell: ({Dc, ch 3} 3 times, dc) in indicated st or sp.

Joining open shell: (Dc, ch 3, dc, ch 1, remove hook from lp, insert hook in corresponding ch-3 sp of open shell on previous Motif, pick up dropped lp, draw through ch-3 sp, ch 1, dc, ch 3, dc) in indicated sp on working Motif.

Joining ch-5 sp (jch-5 sp): Ch 2, remove hook from lp, insert hook in corresponding ch-5 sp on previous Motif, pick up dropped lp, draw through ch-5 sp, ch 2.

INSTRUCTIONS

SCARF

First Motif

Rnd 1 (RS): With CC, ch 4, join with sl st to form ring, ch 4 *(counts as first dc, ch-1)*, [dc in ring, ch 1] 11 times, join with sl st in 3rd ch of beg ch-4. *(12 dc, 12 ch-1 sps)*

Rnd 2: Sl st in first ch-1 sp, ch 1; beg in same sp, (sc, ch 3, sc) in each sp around, join with sl st in beg sc. Fasten off. *(12 ch-3 sps, 24 sc)*

Rnd 3: With RS facing, join MC with sl st in any ch-3 sp, ch 1, sc in same sp, *ch 5, sc in next sp, **open shell** *(see Special Stitches)* in next sp**, sc in next sp, rep from * around, ending last rep at **, join with sl st in beg sc. Fasten off. *(4 ch-5 sps, 4 open shells)*

2nd Motif

Rnds 1 & 2: Rep rnds 1 and 2 of First Motif.

Rnd 3: With RS facing, join MC with sl st in any ch-3 sp, ch 1, sc in same sp, ch 5, sc in next sp, **joining open shell** *(see Special Stitches)* in next sp, sc in next sp, **jch-5 sp** *(see Special Stitches)*, sc in next sp, joining open shell in next sp *(one side joined)*, continue around as for rnd 3 of First Motif.

Rem 14 Motifs

Rnds 1–3: Rep rnds 1–3 of Second Motif.

Border

With RS facing, join MC with sl st in center ch-5 sp at either narrow end of scarf, ch 3 *(counts as first dc throughout)*, 6 dc in same sp, *sc

in next ch-3 sp, 3 sc in next sp, sc in next sp, 5 dc in next ch-5 sp, 5 sc in next ch-3 sp, [dc in joining st between working Motif and next Motif, 5 sc in first ch-3 sp on next Motif, 7 dc in next ch-5 sp, 5 sc in next ch-3 sp] across to last Motif, dc in joining st between next working Motif and last Motif, 5 sc in first ch-3 sp on last Motif, 5 dc in next ch-5 sp, sc in next ch-3 sp, 3 sc in next sp, sc in next ch-3 sp**, 7 dc in next ch-5 sp, rep from * around, ending last rep at **, join with sl st in 3rd ch of beg ch-3. Fasten off.

JACKET

Body

First Motif

Size Small Only

Rnd 1 (RS): With size G hook and CC, ch 4, join with sl st to form ring, ch 4 *(counts as first dc, ch-1)*, [dc in ring, ch 1] 11 times, join with sl st in 3rd ch of beg ch-4. *(12 dc, 12 ch-1 sps)*

Sizes Medium & Large Only

Rnd 1 (RS): With size H [J] hook and CC, ch 4, join with sl st to form ring, ch 1, 12 sc in ring, join with sl st in beg sc. *(12 sc)*

Rnd 2: Ch 4 *(counts as first dc, ch-1)*, [dc in next sc, ch 1] around, join with sl st in 3rd ch of beg ch-4. *(12 dc, 12 ch-1 sps)*

Size X-Large Only

Rnd 1 (RS): With size K hook and CC, ch 4, join to form a ring, ch 2 *(counts as first hdc)*, 11 hdc in ring, join with sl st in 2nd ch of beg ch-2. *(12 hdc)*

Rnd 2: Ch 4 *(counts as first dc, ch-1)*, [dc in next hdc, ch 1] around, join with sl st in 3rd ch of beg ch-4. *(12 dc, 12 ch-1 sps)*

All Sizes

Rnd 2 [3, 3, 3]: Rep rnd 2 of First Motif for Scarf.

Rnd 3 [4, 4, 4]: With RS facing, using size G [H, J, K] hook, rep rnd 3 of First Motif for Scarf.

2nd Motif

Rnds 1–2[3, 3, 3]: Rep rnds 1–2 [3, 3, 3] of First Motif for Jacket.

Rnd 3 [4, 4, 4]: Rep rnd 3 of Second Motif for Scarf.

Rem 52 Motifs

Rnds 1–3[4, 4, 4]: Following Assembly Diagram, rep rnds 1–3 [4, 4, 4] of Second Motif, joining on as many sides as indicated on diagram. Leave armhole openings as indicated on Assembly Diagram. When working 4 Motifs across top strip at shoulder edge, fold 2 Front pieces across Back and join Front to Back at shoulder edge on rnd 3 [4, 4, 4].

Body Edging

With RS facing, join MC with sl st in ch-5 sp at center of Back neck, ch 3 *(counts as first dc)*, 6 dc in same sp, sc in next ch-3 sp, dc in joining between Motifs, sc in next ch-3 sp, 7 dc in next ch-5 sp, 5 sc in next ch-3 sp, *[dc in joining between Motifs, 5 sc in next ch-3 sp, 7 dc in next ch-5 sp, 5 sc in next ch-3 sp]* 4 times, **dc in joining between Motifs, 5 sc in next ch-3 sp, 5 dc in next ch-5 sp, sc in next ch-3 sp, 3 sc in next ch-3 sp, sc in next ch-3 sp, 5 dc in next ch-5 sp, 5 sc in next ch-3 sp**, work bet * 7 times, work bet ** once, work bet * 4 times, dc in joining between Motifs, 5 sc in next ch-3 sp, 7 dc in next ch-5 sp, sc in next ch-3 sp, dc in joining between Motifs, sc in next ch-3 sp, join with sl st in 3rd ch of beg ch-3. Fasten off.

Sleeve

Make 2.

First Motif

Rnds 1–3 [4, 4, 4]: Rep rnds 1–3 [4, 4, 4] of First Motif for Jacket Body.

2nd Motif

Rnds 1–3 [4, 4, 4]: Rep rnds 1–3 [4, 4, 4] of Second Motif for Jacket Body.

Rem 18 Motifs

Rnds 1-3 [4, 4, 4]: Following Assembly Diagram, rep rnds 1–3 [4, 4, 4] of 2nd Motif, joining on as many sides as indicated and always joining last motif on each strip to First Motif to form tube. Join each motif on last strip at top of Sleeve to corresponding motif at armhole opening of Jacket.

Sleeve Edging

With RS facing, join MC with sl st in joining between any 2 Motifs at bottom of either Sleeve, ch 3 *(counts as first dc)*, *5 sc in next ch-3 sp, 7 dc in next ch-5 sp, 5 sc in next ch-3 sp**, dc in joining between 2 Motifs, rep from * around, ending last rep at **, join with sl st in 3rd ch of beg ch-3. Fasten off.

Rep on rem Sleeve. ❑❑

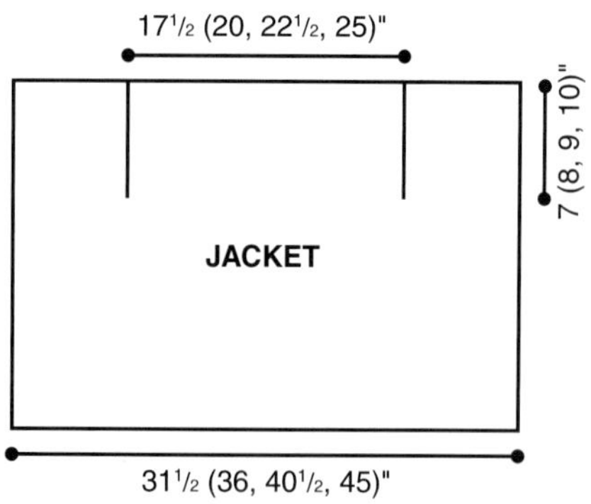

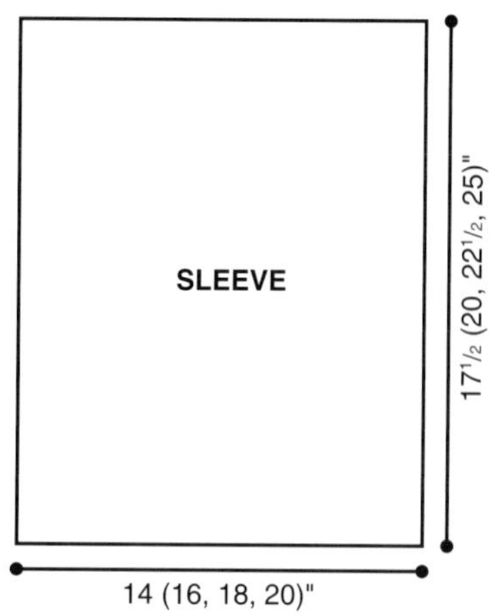

ASSEMBLY DIAGRAM

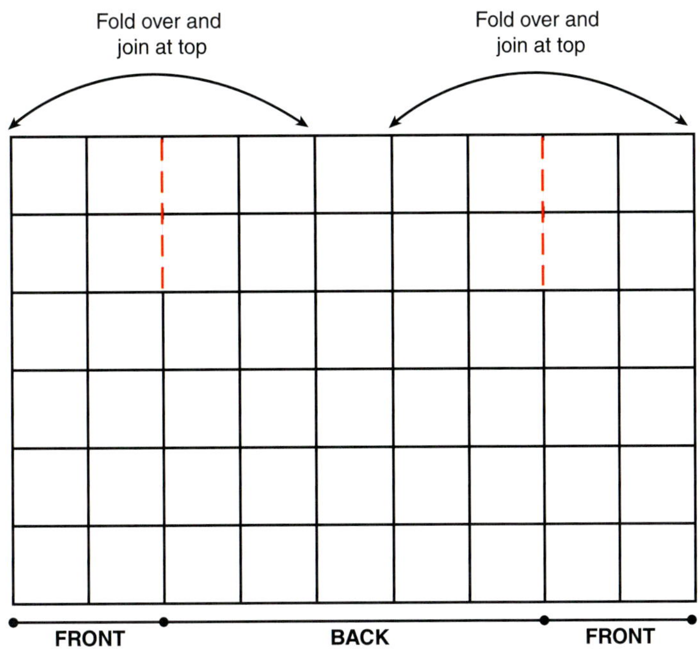

JACKET BODY

STITCH KEY
- - - - Leave open for armholes

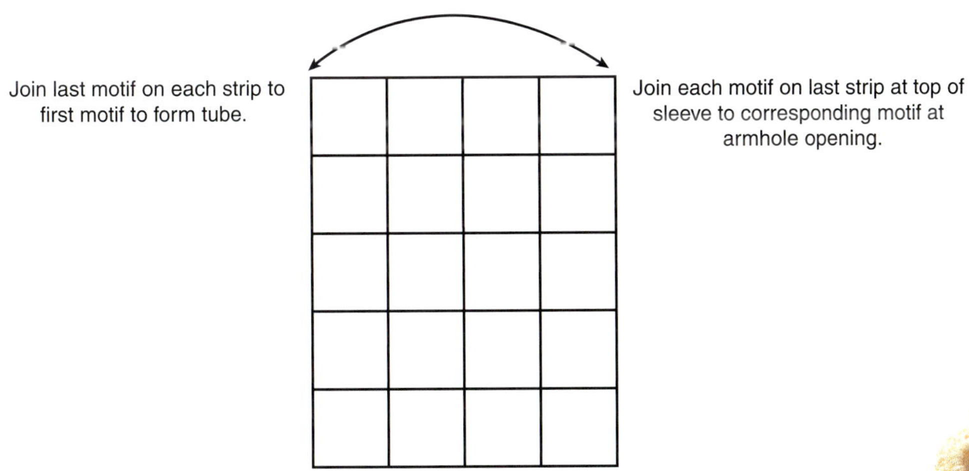

SLEEVE

Ferris Wheel

Designs by Dorothy Drake

SKILL LEVEL

INTERMEDIATE

FINISHED MEASUREMENTS

Afghan: 64 x 42 inches

Rug: 32 inches square without fringe

MATERIALS

- ❑ Red Heart Super Saver medium (worsted) weight yarn (7 oz/364 yds/198g per skein):
  - 5 skeins #312 black *(A)*
  - 3 skeins #311 white *(B)*
  - 1 skein each #319 cherry red *(CC)*, #886 blue *(CC)* #354 vibrant orange *(CC)*, #356 amethyst *(DD)* and #324 bright yellow *(CC)*
- ❑ Red Heart Kids medium (worsted) weight yarn (5 oz/141g/290 yds/265m per skein):
  - 1 skein #2652 lime *(CC)*
- ❑ Sizes I/9/5mm and J/10/6mm crochet hooks or size needed to obtain gauge
- ❑ 12 straight or safety pins (optional)

GAUGE

With size J hook and B: Outer Ring = 5½ inches in diameter

SPECIAL STITCHES

Picot: Ch 2, sl st in last sc made.

Joined treble (jtr): Holding back last lp of each st on hook sk 3 sc on same spoke, tr in next sc, sk first sc on next spoke, tr in next sc, yo, draw through all 3 lps on hook.

Joining chain-3 (jch-3): Ch 1, sc in corresponding ch-3 sp on previous Motif, ch 1.

INSTRUCTIONS

RUG

FIRST LARGE MOTIF

Spokes

Rnd 1 (RS): With size J hook and any CC, ch 4, join with sl st to form ring, ch 1, 12 sc in ring, join with sl st in beg sc. *(12 sc)*

Rnd 2: Ch 1, beg in same sc as joining, (sc, ch 16, sc) in each sc around, join with sl st in beg sc. *(12 ch-16 sps)*

Rnd 3: Sl st in first ch-16 sp, beg in same sp, (8 sc, hdc, 3 dc, ch 3, 3 dc, hdc, 8 sc) in each sp around, join with sl st in beg sc. Fasten off.

Lightly steam or block Motif so that spokes lay flat around.

Outer Ring

Rnd 1 (RS): With size J hook and B, ch 48, join with sl st to form ring, ch 1, beg in same ch as joining, sc in each ch around, join with sl st in beg sc. *(48 sc)*

Rnd 2: Ch 1, sc in same sc as joining, sc in next sc, **picot** *(see Special Stitches)*, [sc in each of next 2 sc, picot] around, join with sl st in beg sc. Fasten off. *(24 picots)*

Inner Ring

Rnd 1 (RS): With size J hook and A, ch 26, join with sl st to form ring, ch 1; beg in same ch as joining, sc in each ch around, join with sl st in beg sc. *(26 sc)*

Rnd 2: Ch 1, sc in same sc as joining, 2 sc in next sc, [sc in each of next 2 sc, 2 sc in next sc] around, join with sl st in beg sc. Fasten off. *(35 sc)*

With RS facing, place Inner Ring on top of Spokes. Draw every other spoke through the center hole of the Inner Ring. Place Outer Ring on top, draw spokes through creating a basket weave pattern. If desired, pin ends of spokes in place when working Border.

Border

Rnd 1 (RS): With RS facing, with size J hook, join A with a sl st in first dc of 3 dc to right of ch-3 sp at top of any spoke, ch 1, sc in same dc, sc in each of next 2 dc, (2 sc, ch 3, 2 sc) in ch-3 sp, sc in each of next 3 dc, ch 1, *sc in next picot on Outer Ring, ch 1**, sc in each of next 3 dc on next spoke, (2 sc, ch 3, 2 sc) in ch-3 sp, sc in each of next 3 dc, ch 1, sk next picot on Outer Ring, rep from * around, ending last rep at **, join with sl st in beg sc.

Rnd 2: Sl st in next sc, ch 8 *(counts as first tr, ch-4)*, *(sc, ch 3, sc) in ch-3 sp at tip of spoke, ch 4**, **jtr** *(see Special Stitches)*, ch 4, rep from * around, ending last rep at **, sk 3 sc, tr in next sc, join with sl st in 4th ch of beg ch-8 to form last jtr. Fasten off.

2ND LARGE MOTIF

Spokes

Rnds 1–3: Rep rnds 1–3 of Spokes for First Large Motif.

Outer Ring

Rnds 1 & 2: Rep rnds 1 and 2 of Outer Ring for First Large Motif.

Inner Ring

Rnds 1 & 2: Rep rnds 1 and 2 for Inner Ring for First Large Motif.

Border

Rnd 1: Rep rnd 1 for Border for First Large Motif.

Rnd 2: Sl st in next sc, ch 8 *(counts as first tr, ch-4)*, [(sc, **jch-3**—*see Special Stitches*, sc) in ch-3 sp at tip of spoke, ch 4, jtr, sl st in next jtr on previous Motif, ch 4] twice, (sc, jch-3, sc) in ch-3 sp at tip of spoke *(1 side joined)*, continue around as for rnd 2 of Border for First Large Motif.

REM 7 LARGE MOTIFS

Rep instructions for 2nd Large Motif, joining on rnd 2 of Border on as many sides as indicated to form 3 rows of 3 Large Motifs each. Leave 2 spokes free between Motif joinings.

FILLER MOTIF

Make 4.

Rnd 1 (RS): With size I hook and B, ch 4, join with sl st to form ring, ch 1, 12 sc in ring, join with sl st in beg sc. *(12 sc)*

Rnd 2: Ch 1; beg in same sc as joining, 2 sc in each sc around, join with sl st in beg sc. *(24 sc)*

Rnd 3: Ch 5; drop B to WS, draw A through lp on hook, sc in next sc, ch 5, *drop A to WS, draw B through lp on hook, sc in next sc, ch 5, drop B to WS, draw A through lp on hook, sc in next sc**, ch 5, rep from * around, ending last rep at **, ch 2, dc at base of beg ch-5 to form last ch-5 sp. Fasten off B only.

Join Filler Motif to Large Motif

Rnd 4: Ch 1, sc in sp just formed, *ch 2, sc in ch-4 sp on Large Motif, ch 2, sk next ch-5 sp on Filler Motif, sc in 3rd ch of next ch-5 , ch 2, sc in next ch-4 sp on Large Motif, ch 2, sk next ch-5 sp on Filler Motif, sc in 3rd ch of next ch-5, ch 2, sc in joining between Large Motifs, ch 2, sk next ch-5 sp on Filler Motif**, sc in 3rd ch of next ch-5, rep from * around, ending last rep at **, join with sl st in beg sc. Fasten off.

Rug Border

Rnd 1 (RS): With RS facing, using size J hook, join A with a sl st in any corner ch-3 sp, ch 1, sc in same sp, ch 5, [sc in next sp, ch 4] around, join with sl st in beg sc.

Rnd 2: Sl st into first sp, ch 2 *(counts as first hdc)*, 3 hdc in same sp, 4 hdc in each rem sp around, join with sl st in 2nd ch of beg ch-2.

Rnd 3: Ch 1, sc in same hdc as joining, ch 4, *drop A to WS, draw B through lp on hook, sc in next hdc, ch 4**, drop B to WS, draw A through lp on hook, sc in next hdc, ch 4, rep from * around, ending last rep at **, join with sl st in beg sc. Fasten off A and B.

Fringe

Cut one 5-inch length of yarn to match color of each st on rnd 3 of Border. Knot one length into each matching color stitch around.

AFGHAN

FIRST LARGE MOTIF

Spokes

Rnds 1–3: Rep rnds 1–3 of Spokes for First Large Motif for Rug.

Outer Ring

Rnds 1 & 2: Rep rnds 1 and 2 of Outer Ring for First Large Motif for Rug.

Inner Ring

Rnds 1 & 2: Rep rnds 1 and 2 of Inner Ring for First Large Motif for Rug.

Border

Rnds 1 & 2: Rep rnds 1 and 2 of Border for First Large Motif for Rug.

2ND LARGE MOTIF

Spokes

Rnds 1–3: Rep rnds 1–3 of Spokes for First Large Motif.

Outer Ring

Rnds 1 & 2: Rep rnds 1 and 2 of Outer Ring for First Large Motif.

Inner Ring

Rnds 1 & 2: Rep rnds 1 and 2 for Inner Ring for First Large Motif.

Border

Rnds 1 & 2: Rep rnds 1 and 2 for Border for 2nd Large Motif for Rug.

REM 22 LARGE MOTIFS

Rep instructions for 2nd Large Motif, joining on rnd 2 of Border on as many sides as indicated to form 6 rows of 4 Large Motifs each. Leave 2 spokes free between Motif joinings.

FILLER MOTIF

Make 15.

Rnd 1 (RS): With size I hook and B, ch 4, join with sl st to form ring, ch 1, 12 sc in ring, join with sl st in beg sc. *(12 sc)*

Rnd 2: Ch 1; beg in same sc as joining, 2 sc in each sc around, join with sl st in beg sc. *(24 sc)*

Rnd 3: Ch 5; drop B to WS, draw A through lp on hook, sc in next sc, ch 5, *drop A to WS, draw B through lp on hook, sc in next sc, ch 5, drop B to WS, draw A through lp on hook, sc in next sc**, ch 5, rep from * around, ending last rep at **, ch 2, dc at base of beg ch-5 to form last ch-5 sp. Fasten off B only.

Join Filler Motif to Large Motif

Rnd 4: Ch 1, sc in sp just formed, *ch 2, sc in ch-4 sp on Large Motif, ch 2, sk next ch-5 sp on Filler Motif, sc in 3rd ch of next ch-5 , ch 2, sc in next ch-4 sp on Large Motif, ch 2, sk next ch-5 sp on Filler Motif, sc in 3rd ch of next ch-5, ch 2, sc in joining between Large Motifs, ch 2, sk next ch-5 sp on Filler Motif**, sc in 3rd ch of next ch-5, rep from * around, ending last rep at **, join with sl st in beg sc. Fasten off.

Outer Edger Filler Motif

Make 16.

Rnd 1 (RS): With size I hook and B, ch 1 *(center ch)*, ch 3 more *(counts as first dc)*, 11 dc in center ch, join with sl st in 3rd ch of beg ch-3. Fasten off. *(12 dc)*

Rnd 2: With RS facing, join A with a sl st in any dc, ch 1, sc in same dc, [ch 2, sk next dc, sc in next dc] 3 times, ch 2, sc in ch-4 sp between joining of any 2 Large Motifs on outer edge of afghan, ch 2, sk next dc of working Motif, sc in next dc, ch 2, sc in joining between 2 Large Motifs, ch 2, sk next dc, sc in next dc on working Motif, ch 2, sc in next ch-4 sp on next Large Motif, ch 2, sk next dc, join with sl st in beg sc. Fasten off.

Afghan Border

Rnds 1–3: Rep rnds 1–3 of Rug Border. ❑❑

Denim Blues

Designs by Cindy Carlson

SKILL LEVEL

INTERMEDIATE

FINISHED MEASUREMENTS

Hat: 21 inches x 9 inches

Scarf: 9 inches x 53 inches

MATERIALS

- ❑ Red Heart Super Saver medium (worsted) weight yarn (3 oz/85g/160 yds per skein): 4 MEDIUM
  - 3 skeins #311 white *(MC)*
- ❑ Red Heart Classic medium (worsted) weight yarn (3 oz/85g/167 yds per skein): 4 MEDIUM
  - 3 skeins #974 country blues *(CC)*
- ❑ Size 8/H/5mm crochet hook or size needed to obtain gauge
- ❑ Yarn needle

GAUGE

6 dc = 2 inches

2 rows dc = 1 inch

SPECIAL STITCHES

Roll stitch (roll st): Yo 7 times, insert hook in indicated st or sp, yo, draw up a lp, yo, draw through all lps on hook, ch 1 to secure.

Surface chain (surface ch): Holding yarn on WS of work, insert hook from RS to WS between any 2 sts on indicated row, yo, draw up a lp to RS of work, [insert hook between next 2 sts, yo, draw up lp to RS of work and through lp on hook] across to end of row. Fasten off.

INSTRUCTIONS

HAT

Motif

Make 7.

Rnd 1 (RS): With CC, ch 5, join with sl st to form ring, ch 3, 12 **roll sts** *(see Special Stitches)* in ring, join with sl st in top of first roll st. Fasten off. *(12 roll sts)*

Rnd 2: With RS facing, join MC with a sl st between any 2 roll sts, ch 1, 2 sc in same sp, 2 sc between same roll st and next roll st, *(2 sc, ch 2, 2 sc) between same roll st and next roll st,**, [2 sc between same roll st and next roll st] twice, rep from * around, ending last rep at **, join with sl st in beg sc. Fasten off. *(32 sc, 4 ch-2 sps)*

Crown

Row 1 (RS): With RS facing, join MC with a sl st in any corner ch-2 sp of any Motif, ch 1, sc in same sp, *sc in each of next 8 sc, sc in next ch-2 sp**, sc in any ch-2 sp on next Motif, rep from * across until 7 Motifs have been joined, ending last rep at **, turn. *(70 sc)*

Row 2: Ch 1, sc in each sc across, turn.

Row 3: Ch 3 *(counts as first dc throughout)*, dc in each rem sc across, turn. *(70 dc)*

Row 4: Ch 3, dc in next dc, **bpdc** *(see Stitch Guide)* in each of next 2 dc, dc in each of next 2 dc, bpdc in each of next 2 dc, [dc in each of next 4 dc, bpdc in each of next 2 dc, dc in each of next 2 dc, bpdc in each of next 2 dc] across, ending with dc in each of last 2 dc, turn. *(70 sts)*

Row 5: Ch 3, dc in each dc, **fpdc** *(see Stitch Guide)* in each bpdc across, turn.

Row 6: Ch 3, dc in each dc, bpdc in each fpdc across, turn.

Rows 7 & 8: Rep rows 5 and 6.

Rows 9–13: Ch 1, sc in each st across, turn. At end of row 13, fasten off, leaving length for finishing. *(70 sc)*

Surface Chain

With RS facing, work **surface ch** *(see Special Stitches)* with CC over rows 2, 9, and 11.

Finishing

With yarn needle, weave length left for finishing through sc sts of last row, pull tightly tog, sew down side of hat to top of Motifs. Fasten off.

Bottom Border

Rnd 1: With RS facing, join MC with sl st in ch-2 sp at bottom of Motif at back seam, ch 1; beg in same sp, sc in each sc and each ch-2 sp around, join with sl st in beg sc. *(70 sc)*

Rnd 2: Ch 1, sc in same sc as joining, sc in each rem sc around. Fasten off.

Rnd 3: With RS facing, join CC with a sl st in same st as joining, ch 1, sl st in each rem sc around, join with sl st in beg sl st. Fasten off.

Tassel

With CC, ch 1 *(center ch)*, (ch 16, {sl st, ch 10, sl st} in center ch) 5 times. Fasten off, leaving short length for finishing.

With yarn needle and length left for finishing, sew Tassel to top of hat.

SCARF

Motif

Make 18.

Rnds 1 & 2: Rep rnds 1 and 2 of Motif for hat.

First Half of Body

Row 1 (RS): Beg at lower edge, with RS facing, join MC with a sl st in any corner ch-2 sp of any Motif, ch 1, sc in same sp, *sc in each of next 8 sc, sc in next ch-2 sp**, sc in any ch-2 sp on next Motif, rep from * across until 3 Motifs have been joined, ending last rep at **, turn. *(30 sc)*

Row 2: Ch 3 *(counts as first dc throughout)*, dc in each sc across, turn. *(30 dc)*

Row 3: Ch 3, dc in next dc, fpdc in each of next 2 dc, dc in each of next 2 dc, fpdc in each of next 2 dc, [dc in each of next 4 dc, fpdc in each of next 2 dc, dc in each of next 2 dc, fpdc in each of next 2 dc] twice, dc in each of last 2 dc, turn. *(30 sts)*

Row 4: Ch 3, dc in each rem dc, bpdc in each fpdc across, turn.

Row 5: Ch 3, dc in each rem dc, fpdc in each bpdc across, turn.

Row 6: Rep row 4.

Row 7: Working through both thicknesses of last row and any Motif at the same time, ch 1, sc in first st of last row and ch-2 sp on any Motif, *sc in each of next 8 sts on last row and 8 sc of Motif, sc in next st on last row and in ch-2 sp of Motif**, sc in next st on last row and first ch-2 sp on next Motif, rep from * across until 3 Motifs have been joined, ending last rep at **. Fasten off.

Row 8: Working across opposite sides of Motifs just joined, rep row 1 of Upper Hat across 3 Motifs. *(30 sc)*

Rows 9–15: Rep rows 2–8.

Rows 16–18: Rep rows 2–4.

Rows 19–27: Rep rows 5 and 6 alternately, ending with a row 5.

Rows 28-30: Ch 1, sc in each st across, turn. At end of row 30, fasten off. *(30 sc)*

2nd Half of Body

Rows 1-30: Rep rows 1-30 of First Half of Body.

Bottom Border

Row 1: With RS facing, join MC with a sl st in first ch-2 sp of Motif at bottom of First Half of Body, rep row 1 of Upper Hat across 3 Motifs. *(30 sc)*

Row 2: Ch 1, sc in each sc across. Fasten off.

Rep at bottom of Second Half of Body.

Fringe

With RS facing, join CC with a sl st in **front lp** *(see Stitch Guide)* only of first sc on row 2 of Bottom Border of First Half of Body; working in front lps only across, *ch 10, sl st in same st as last sl st made**, sl st in next st, rep from * across to last st, ending last rep at **, turn; working in rem lps across same row, sl st in first st, +ch 16, sl st in same st as last sl st made++, sl st in next st, rep from + across to last st, ending last rep at ++. Fasten off.

Rep on Bottom Border of 2nd Half of Body.

Join First and 2nd Halves of Body

With WS tog, working through both thicknesses of First and 2 Half of Body at the same time, join CC with a sl st in first st of row 30, [ch 1, sl st in next st] across. Fasten off.

Finishing

With CC, work surface ch across rows 1, 8, 15, 28 and 29 on First and 2nd Halves of Body. ❑❑

English Rose Table Set

Designs by Tammy Hildebrand

SKILL LEVEL

INTERMEDIATE

FINISHED MEASUREMENTS

Table Runner: 38½ inches x 10½ inches
Placemat: 17½ inches x 10½ inches
Coaster: 3½ inches square

MATERIALS

- ❑ J & P Coats Crochet Nylon 3-ply size 18 crochet thread (150 yds/137m per tube):
  2 tubes each #1 white *(A)*, #52 pink *(B)* and #38 celery *(C)*
- ❑ Size I/9/5.5mm crochet hook or size needed to obtain gauge

GAUGE

First Motif = 3½ inches square

SPECIAL STITCHES

Bobble: Holding back last lp of each st on hook, work 3 dc in indicated sp or st, yo, draw through all 4 lps on hook.

Beginning bobble (beg bobble): (Ch 3, holding back last lp of each st on hook, work 2 dc, yo, draw through all 3 lps on hook) in indicated st or sp.

Shell: (3 dc, ch 2, 3 dc) in indicated st or sp.

Beginning shell (beg shell): (Ch 3, 2 dc, ch 2, 3 dc) in indicated st or sp.

Picot: Ch 2, sc in 2nd ch from hook.

Joining ch-3 sp (jch-3 sp): Ch 1, sl st in corresponding ch-3 sp on previous Motif, ch 1.

INSTRUCTIONS

COASTER

Motif

Rnd 1 (RS): With B, ch 4, join with sl st to form ring, **beg bobble** *(see Special Stitches)* in ring, ch 1, (**bobble**—*see Special Stitches*, ch 1) 7 times in ring, join with sl st in top of beg bobble. Fasten off. *(8 bobbles, 8 ch-1 sps)*

Rnd 2: With RS facing, join A with a sl st in any ch-1 sp, **beg shell** *(see Special Stitches)* in same sp, *3 dc in next sp**, **shell** *(see Special Stitches)* in next sp, rep from * around, ending last rep at **, join with sl st in 3rd ch of beg ch-3. Fasten off. *(4 shells, 4 3-dc groups)*

Rnd 3: With RS facing, join C with a sl st in any shell sp, ch 1, (sc, ch 3, sc) in same sp, *ch 1, [sk next dc, sc in next dc, ch 1] 4 times, sk next dc**, (sc, ch 3, sc) in shell sp, rep from * around, ending last rep at **, join with sl st in beg sc. Fasten off. *(4 ch-3 sps, 20 ch-1 sps)*

Coaster Edging

With RS facing, join A with a sl st in any sp, **picot** *(see Special Stitches)*, (sl st, picot) in each rem sp around, join with sl st in beg sc. Fasten off.

PLACEMAT

First Motif

Rnds 1–3: Rep rnds 1–3 of Motif for Coaster.

2nd Motif

Rnds 1 & 2: Rep rnds 1 and 2 of First Motif.

Rnd 3: With RS facing, join C with a sl st in any shell sp, ch 1, (sc, **jch-3 sp**—*see Special Stitches*, sc) in same sp, ch 1, sl st in next ch-1 sp on previous Motif, [sk next dc on working Motif, sc in next dc, ch 1, sl st in next sp on previous Motif] 4 times, (sc, jch-3 sp, sc) in next shell sp on working Motif *(one side joined)*, continue around as for rnd 3 of First Motif.

Rem 13 Motifs

Rnds 1–3: Rep rnds 1–3 of 2nd Motif, joining on as many sides as necessary to form 3 rows of 5 Motifs each.

Placemat Edging

With RS facing, join A with a sl st in any sp, picot, (sl st, picot) in each rem sp and in each joining between Motifs around, join with sl st in beg sc. Fasten off.

TABLE RUNNER

First Motif

Rnds 1–3: Rep rnds 1–3 of Motif for Placemat.

2nd Motif

Rnds 1 & 2: Rep rnds 1 and 2 of First Motif for Placemat.

Rnd 3: Rep rnd 3 of 2nd Motif for Placemat.

Rem 31 Motifs

Rnds 1–3: Rep rnds 1–3 of 2nd Motif, joining on as many sides as necessary to form 3 rows of 11 Motifs each.

Table Runner Edging

Rep instructions for Placemat Edging. ❑❑

Stitch Guide

ABBREVIATIONS

beg .... begin/beginning
bpdc .... back post double crochet
bpsc .... back post single crochet
bptr .... back post treble crochet
CC .... contrasting color
ch .... chain stitch
ch- .... refers to chain or space previously made (i.e. ch-1 space)
ch sp .... chain space
cl .... cluster
cm .... centimeter(s)
dc .... double crochet
dec .. decrease/decreases/decreasing
dtr .... double treble crochet
fpdc .... front post double crochet
fpsc .... front post single crochet
fptr .... front post treble crochet
g .... gram(s)
hdc .... half double crochet
inc .... increase/increases/increasing
lp(s) .... loop(s)
MC .... main color
mm .... millimeter(s)
oz .... ounce(s)
pc .... popcorn
rem .... remain/remaining
rep .... repeat(s)
rnd(s) .... round(s)
RS .... right side
sc .... single crochet
sk .... skip(ped)
sl st .... slip stitch
sp(s) .... space(s)
st(s) .... stitch(es)
tog .... together
tr .... treble crochet
trtr .... triple treble
WS .... wrong side
yd(s) .... yard(s)
yo .... yarn over

Chain—ch: Yo, pull through lp on hook.

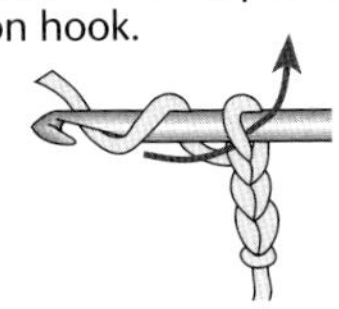

Slip stitch—sl st: Insert hook in st, yo, pull through both lps on hook.

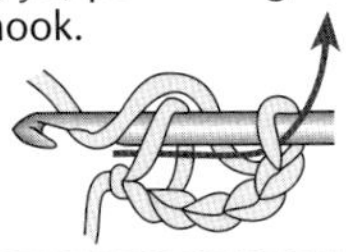

Single crochet—sc: Insert hook in st, yo, pull through st, yo, pull through both lps on hook.

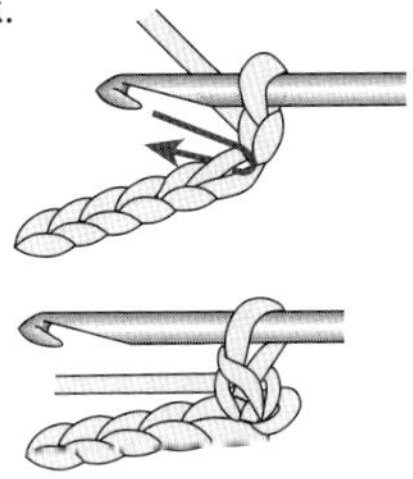

Front loop—front lp
Back loop—back lp

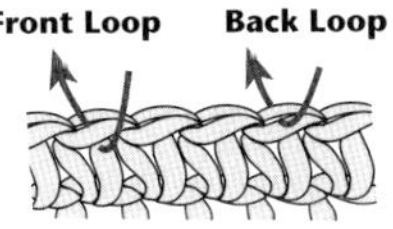

Front post stitch—fp:
Back post stitch—bp: When working post st, insert hook from right to left around post st on previous row.

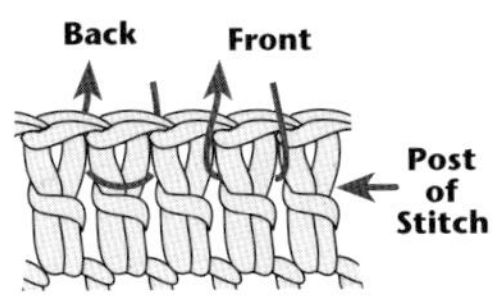

Half double crochet—hdc: Yo, insert hook in st, yo, pull through st, yo, pull through all 3 lps on hook.

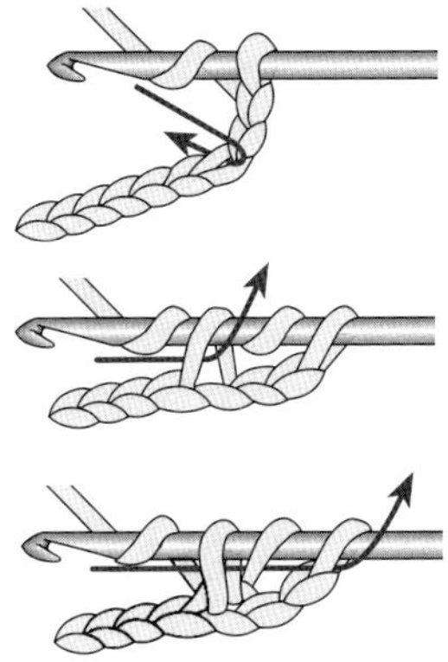

Double crochet—dc: Yo, insert hook in st, yo, pull through st, [yo, pull through 2 lps] twice.

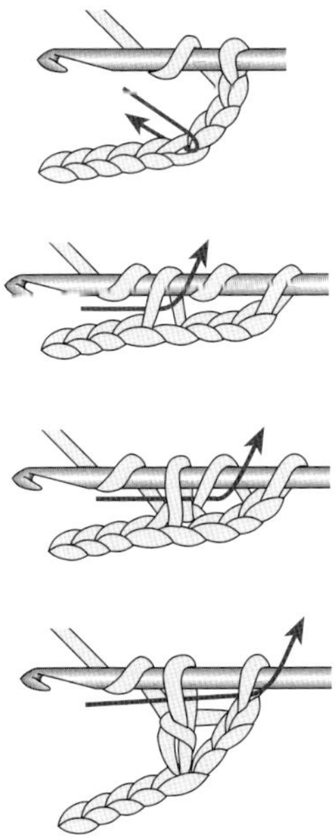

Change colors: Drop first color; with 2nd color, pull through last 2 lps of st.

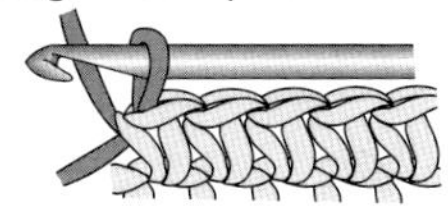

Treble crochet—tr: Yo 2 times, insert hook in st, yo, pull through st, [yo, pull through 2 lps] 3 times.

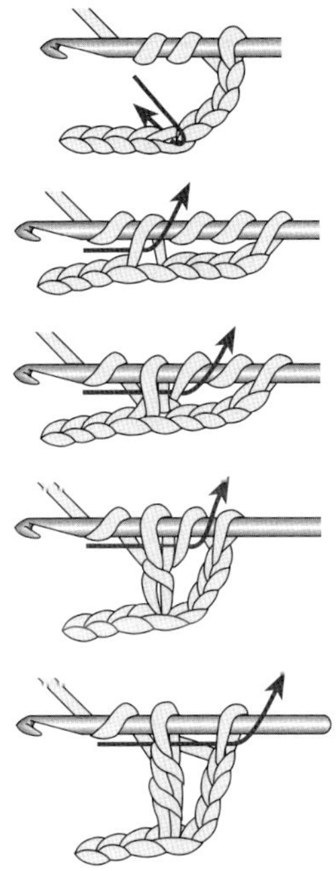

Double treble crochet—dtr: Yo 3 times, insert hook in st, yo, pull through st, [yo, pull through 2 lps] 4 times.

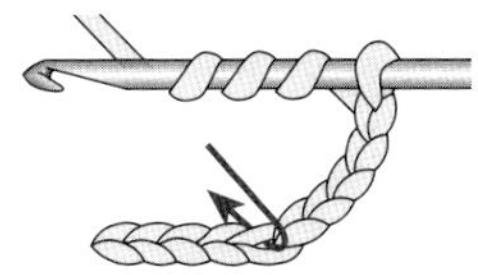

Single crochet decrease (sc dec): (Insert hook, yo, draw up a lp) in each of the sts indicated, yo, draw through all lps on hook.

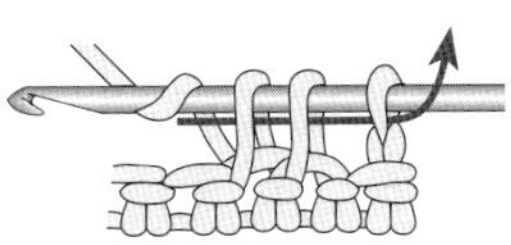

Example of 2-sc dec

Half double crochet decrease (hdc dec): (Yo, insert hook, yo, draw lp through) in each of the sts indicated, yo, draw through all lps on hook.

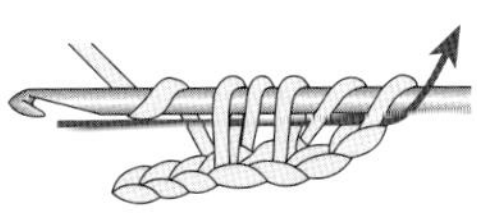

Example of 2-hdc dec

Double crochet decrease (dc dec): (Yo, insert hook, yo, draw lp through, yo, draw through 2 lps on hook) in each of the sts indicated, yo, draw through all lps on hook.

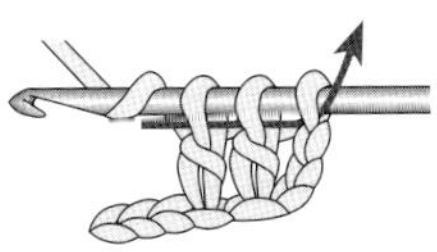

Example of 2-dc dec

US		UK
sl st (slip stitch)	=	sc (single crochet)
sc (single crochet)	=	dc (double crochet)
hdc (half double crochet)	=	htr (half treble crochet)
dc (double crochet)	=	tr (treble crochet)
tr (treble crochet)	=	dtr (double treble crochet)
dtr (double treble crochet)	=	ttr (triple treble crochet)
skip	=	miss

For more complete information, visit

AnniesAttic.com

Annie's Attic®

306 East Parr Road
Berne, IN 46711

TOLL-FREE ORDER LINE or to request a free catalog (800) LV-ANNIE (800) 582-6643
Customer Service (800) AT-ANNIE (800) 282-6643, **Fax** (800) 882-6643
Visit www.AnniesAttic.com

ISBN-10: 1-59635-086-5 ISBN-13: 978-1-59635-086-1

 Printed in USA 1 2 3 4 5 6 7 8 9